WORKBOOK

Kent Kennan

Professor Emeritus of Music,
The University of Texas at Austin

THE TECHNIQUE OF ORCHESTRATION

Sixth Edition

KENT KENNAN
DONALD GRANTHAM

PRENTICE HALL, UPPER SADDLE RIVER, NEW JERSEY 07458

Preface

Most teachers who have used the author's text, THE TECHNIQUE OF ORCHESTRATION, have also used either ORCHESTRATION WORKBOOK I (1952) or ORCHESTRATION WORKBOOK II (1969), or both of these, alternating them on a yearly basis. In an effort to find out which workbook (and which assignments in each) had proved most successful, the author queried a number of teachers. The replies seemed to indicate that each workbook contained particular material that had proved especially valuable. As one teacher put it, "No matter which one I use, I find there is something in the other that I would like to assign." On the theory that there may be other orchestration teachers who share this sentiment, the main objective here has been to assemble in one volume those exercises from both earlier workbooks that seem most instructive. In addition, fourteen new exercises are included. By eliminating blank pages, it was possible to provide considerably more material in this workbook than in the earlier ones. Regrettably, copyright restrictions once again prevented the inclusion of certain contemporary music that the author would have liked to use.

The exercises are arranged in an overall sequence that corresponds with the order of presentation in THE TECHNIQUE OF ORCHESTRATION, sixth edition, by Kent Kennan and Donald Grantham (Prentice Hall, 2002); they are listed in the Table of Contents that follows, along with references to the particular chapters for which they may best serve as assignments. Some lend themselves to scoring for other orchestral groups as well, and these alternative possibilities are also indicated. There is no intention that any one class should do all the exercises in each section. In the case of the more basic assignments, each type is presented twice, with a different musical basis each time. This plan allows for some variation in material assigned from year to year. As for the other less elementary material, each instructor must of course choose whichever exercises seem best suited to his students' needs and abilities. Most of the assignments are aimed at the student in a first-year orchestration course, but some in the last portion of the workbook are of a difficulty that may make them more suitable for an advanced course.

The assignments are arranged in two different formats: (1) the music is given in its original form at the bottom of the page with blank staves above on which the scoring is to be done; (2) the music alone is given, the scoring to be done on a separate sheet. The first arrangement has the advantage of saving the student considerable time that he would otherwise spend in setting up the page; the second assures his learning the correct placement of instruments on the page and the general mechanics of score writing.

The author is deeply grateful to Dr. Donald Grantham for his help in compiling this workbook.

Kent Kennan

0-13-040773-9

0-13-040773-9
18 17 16 15 14 13 12 V036

Table of Contents

In cases where a piece of music lends itself to scoring for orchestral groups other than the one under which it is listed here, the alternative possibilities are indicated by means of letters: W = woodwinds; B = brass; S = strings; WHS = woodwinds, horns , and strings; O = orchestra, including trumpets and/trombones. Thus, "(S,O)" after a title listed under woodwinds means that the music is also suitable for an assignment in scoring for strings or for orchestra.

*The complete work. Only excerpts are given in other cases.

*The complete work. Only excerpts are given in other cases.

Score one of the excerpts below (as specified by the instructor) for strings in six different ways. Use examples 3–6 and 8–11 in Chapter III of the text as general models. It is not necessary to rewrite the clef, key signature, meter signature, or tempo indication in versions 2, 3, 5, and 6. In version 6, make plentiful use of octave doublings. No bowing indications need be included. Tempo markings and dynamics in parentheses were added for purposes of this assignment.

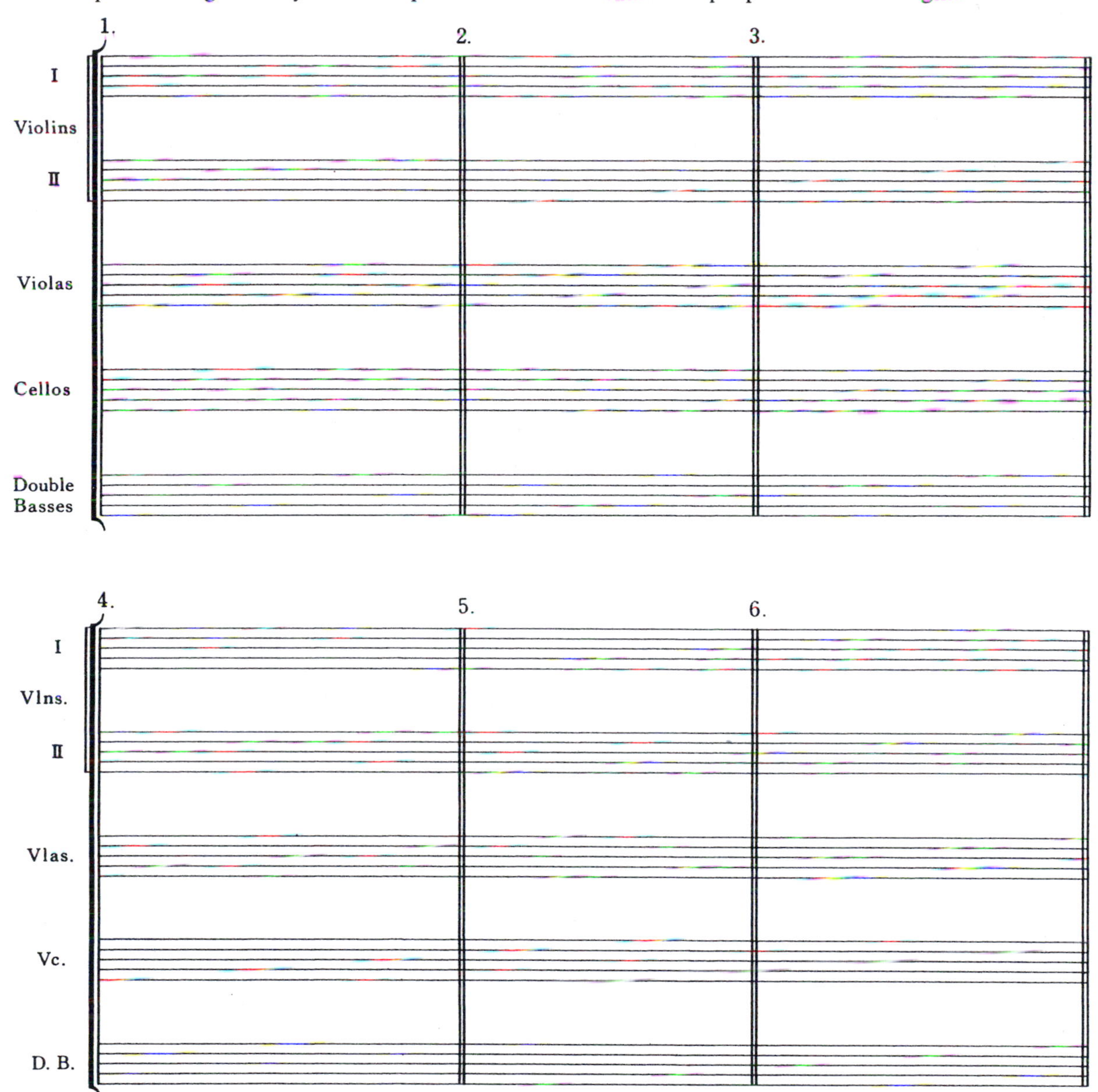

Score for strings. Dynamics will have to be added, since none are included in the original; they should reflect the *espressivo* character of the music without producing an over-romantic effect. The F# and Eb half notes in measure 12 and the F# quarter note in measure 15 are best moved up an octave for reasons of consistent voice-leading and range of instruments. It is suggested that the instructor discuss the question of octave doublings as it applies here, also that of characteristic Baroque bowing. (Bowing indications should be included.)

SARABANDE

From the First French Suite

EXERCISES IN BOWING AND IN THE USE OF ALTO AND TENOR CLEFS

Each of the following fragments is given first with the phrasing used in the original (piano) version, and on the staff below without phrasing. To this latter version, add bowing indications (slurs, up-bow and down-bow signs where necessary, etc.). Aim at the general effect of the original. Exercises 5 to 8 also involve writing the melody in the clef shown. In Exercise 9, observe the transposition used by the double bass, in writing the part.

SONATA IN C MAJOR
Haydn
Allegro (♩. = 63)
5
mf
ff
Viola
SONATA IN B MINOR
Liszt
Allegro energico
6
fff pesante
p non legato
Viola
SONATA PATHÉTIQUE, OP. 13
Beethoven
Adagio cantabile (♩ = 60)
7
p sempre legatiss.
p
p
espress.
Cello
ETUDE, OP. 10, No. 7
Chopin
Lento (♩ = 66)
8
p
Cello
SONATA, OP. 10, No. 2
Beethoven
Allegro (♩ = 108)
9
p cresc.
f
Double Bass

EXERCISES IN BOWING AND IN THE USE OF ALTO AND TENOR CLEFS

The following fragments are given with the phrasing or slurring used in the original (piano) version. Write each passage on the staff below it and add bowing indications—slurs, up-bow and down-bow signs where necessary, etc. Aim at the effect of the original. In the exercise for the double bass, be sure to write the part an octave higher than the concert sounds shown.

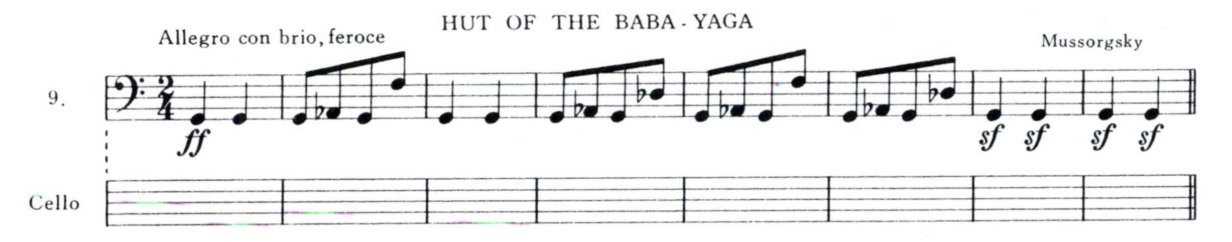

Following are fragments from orchestral works with bowing slurs deleted. Add slurs and any other appropriate bowing indications. Then refer, via the index, to the full-score examples of the same measures given in the text and inspect the bowing specified by the composers. If your version differs from the latter, that does not necessarily mean that it is "wrong." This exercise (which will not be graded), simply aims to acquaint students with bowing patterns considered most effective by composers, in particular musical situations.

Include bowing indications. The instructor should discuss the voice-leading in measures 5 and 6.

SONATA IN B♭ MAJOR (continued)

EXERCISE IN ERROR DETECTION (STRING SCORING)

The scoring here contains a number of errors that occur frequently in students' first work in arranging for strings. On this sheet (or orally in class) point out the errors. Score the excerpt for strings if the instructor so directs.

Score for strings. Analyze the voice-leading carefully before beginning the scoring. Division of the cellos (half on the lower octave of the inner-voice melody and half on the bass) will be necessary in mm. 1–8; there the two lines are best written on separate staves. Divisi passages in other string groups may be written on the same staff.

Score for strings.

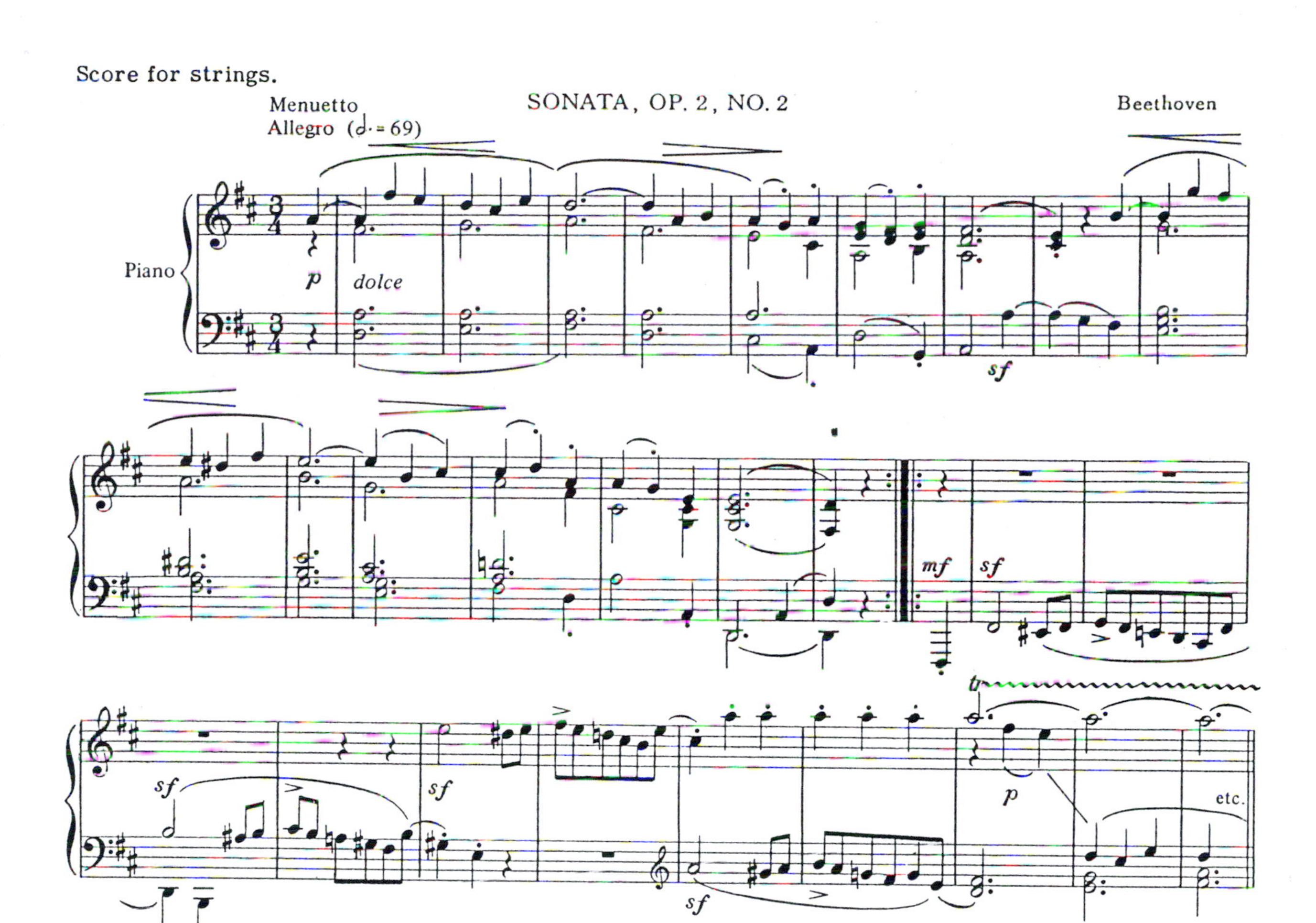

Score for strings. The instructor should discuss the voice leading a suitable scoring of the rolled chords in measures 6 and 7.

Score for strings. Analyze first, noting important melodic elements that recur.

EXERCISE IN ERROR DETECTION (WOODWIND SCORING)

The scoring here contains a number of errors that occur frequently in students' first work in arranging for woodwinds. In the blanks at the bottom of the page, list the error or errors that occur at each corresponding circled number in the music. Points to look for include omission or incorrect use of "1." or "2." or "a2," instruments written out of their range, poor balance, failure to transpose the part, rests missing, linear flaws, etc. This exercise may be done orally in class but in any case should be undertaken before the first assignment in scoring for woodwinds.

1.
2. Out of range
3.
4. which type of clarinet?
5.
6.
7.
8.
9.
10.
11.
12.
13.
14.
15.
16.
17. not a filled measure
18. not needed

Score for woodwinds in pairs.

First look over the entire piece, noting any passages that will have to be taken by particular instruments because of the range involved. Then plot the scoring. In bars 9–16, use quarter notes or dotted half notes in the bottom voice in order to approximate the sustained effect that the pedal gives in the piano version.

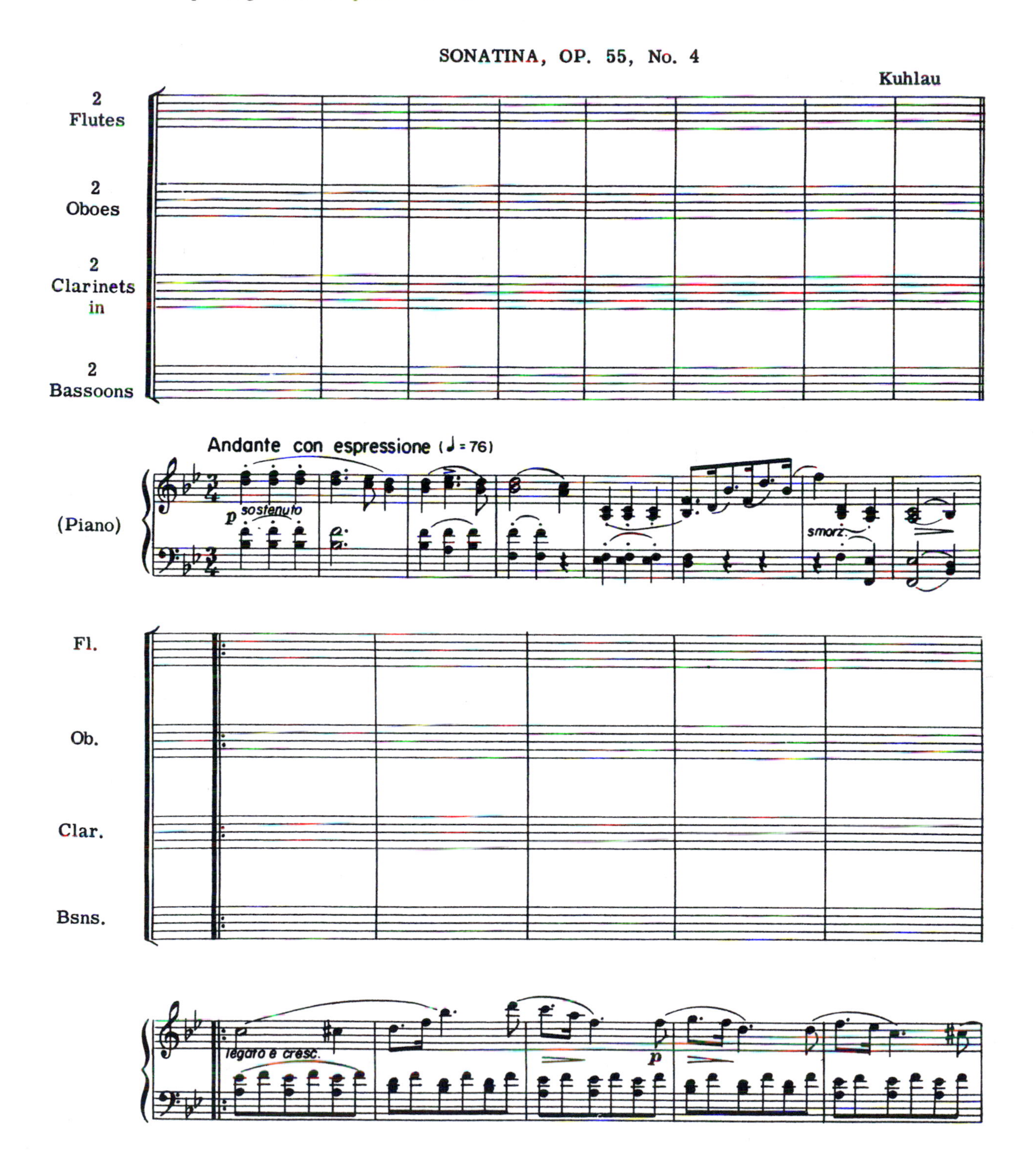

Fl.
Ob.
Clar.
Bsns.
dim.
Fl.
Ob.
Clar.
Bsns.
pp

Score for woodwinds in pairs.

SONATA, OP. 2, NO. 3

Score for woodwinds in pairs.

Expand the original version by doubling the soprano and bass an octave lower and the soprano, alto, and tenor an octave higher. (The upper-octave doubling of the soprano in the piccolo will sound two octaves higher than in the original.) On another sheet, sketch the scoring of the first measure or so at actual pitch before writing the orchestration in transposed form on this page.

Score for flute, oboe, English horn, clarinet, bass clarinet, and bassoon. This piece is also suitable for an assignment in scoring for strings.

EXERCISE IN CONVERTING PARTS FOR HORNS AND TRUMPETS IN VARIOUS KEYS TO CONCERT PITCHES

Below each of the following excerpts from orchestral horn and trumpet parts write the passage as it will actually sound. Include a key signature except in the case of the Strauss and Scriabin examples. This exercise does not attempt to exhaust all the key possibilities for horns and trumpets; but it does include those most often encountered in the study of orchestral scores of the past.

LEONORE No.3 OVERTURE
Beethoven
Horns
in C
VARIATIONS ON A THEME
OF HAYDN
Brahms
Horns
in B♭
basso
SYMPHONY
Franck
Trumpets
in F
DON JUAN
Strauss
Trumpets
in E
POEM OF ECSTASY
Scriabin
Trumpets
in B♭
a2
OVERTURE TO OBERON
Weber
Trumpets
in D

Score the chorale excerpt below for each of the brass groups shown. In the case of the third one, base the scoring on the "expanded version," which achieves greater fullness by doubling the soprano and the bass at the lower octave.

O HAUPT VOLL BLUT UND WUNDEN

Transpose to a higher key and double the melody and bass an octave lower. Make a preliminary sketch of the scoring in the new key, on the staves provided for that purpose.

AMERICA

Score for 2 horns, 2 B♭ trumpets, and 2 trombones.

DAMON AND PHILLIS
From
Canzonets or Little Short Airs
to Five and Six Voices*

[In quick time]

Morley

Soprano [f]
Alto [f] [mf]
Tenor [f]
Tenor [f] [mf]
Bass [f] [mf]

Sop. [mf]
Alt.
Ten. [mf]
Ten.
Bas.

* Words omitted here

Score for brass (four horns, two trumpets, three trombones, and tuba).

Score for brass (2 or 4 horns, 2 trumpets, 3 trombones, tuba). Transposition of the piece down a half step results in a more comfortable key for B♭ trumpets but detracts somewhat from the brilliant effect. If the original key is retained and if B♭ trumpets are used, their part should be spelled enharmonically from measure 8 on.

This excerpt is also suitable for an assignment in scoring for orchestra.

WAR SONG
From
Album for the Young

Score for brass (4 horns, 3 trumpets, 3 trombones, tuba). Compare your completed scoring with Ravel's. This excerpt is also suitable for an assignment in scoring for orchestra.

PROMENADE
From
Pictures at an Exhibition

Score for brass (4 horns, 3 trumpets, 3 trombones, tuba). Consider the use of mutes.

This piece is also suitable for an assignment in scoring for woodwinds, horns, and strings.

FOLK SONG No. 8
From
Ten Easy Pieces for Piano

These chords are given in basic four-voice form. In scoring them, octave doublings are to be added wherever appropriate, but the chord members now in bass and soprano should be retained; for example, in the second chord below, a G (in whatever octave is desired) should be the top note, and a C should be the bottom note. In scoring brass, be sure to observe the principles of balance discussed in the text.

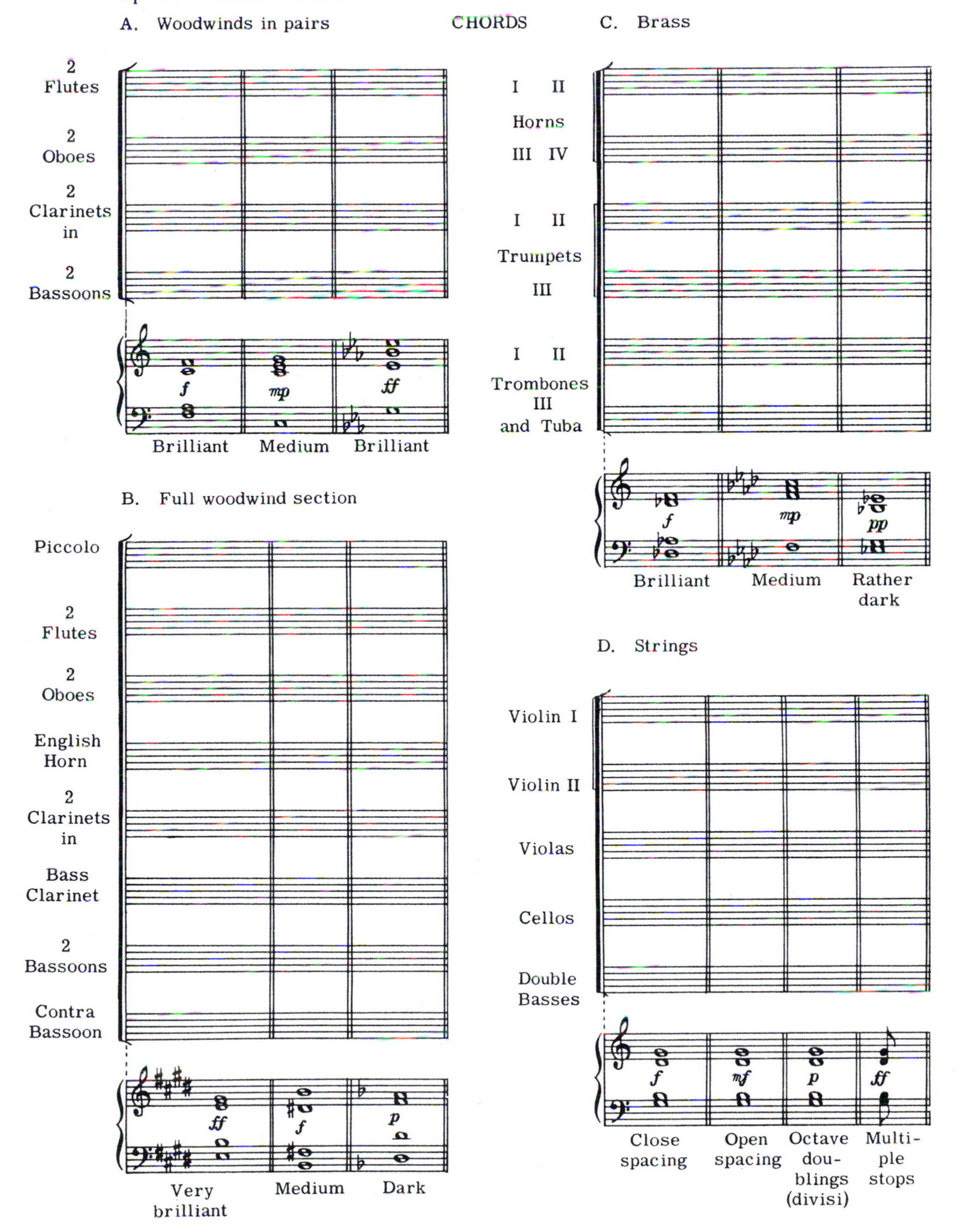

CHORDS (continued)

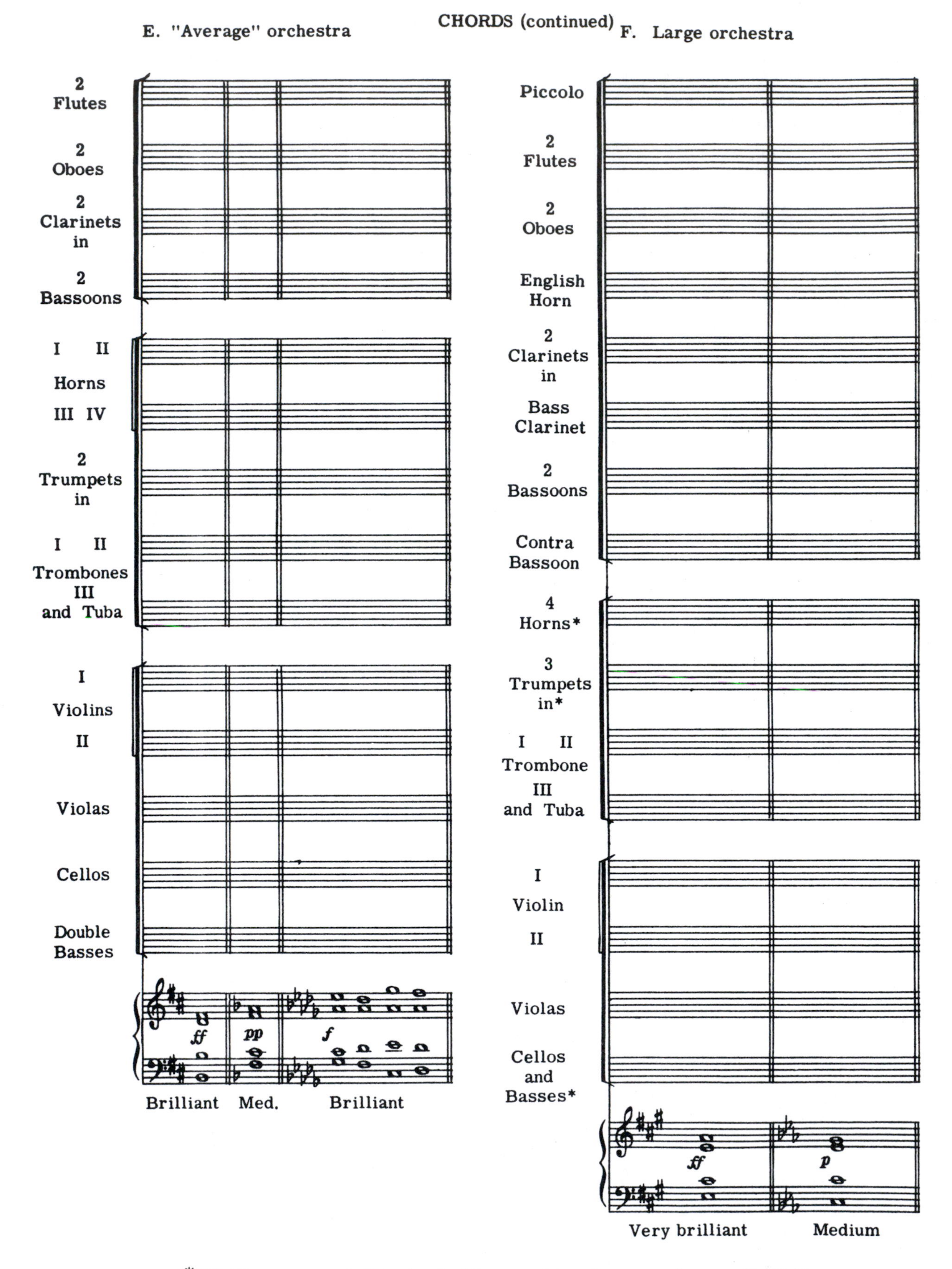

* Written on one staff instead of the usual two because of space limitations.

These chords are given in basic four-voice form, some with a key signature and some with accidentals instead. When a key signature is used in the original version, write the appropriate key signature in the part for each instrument; when no key signature appears in the original, use none in the scored version but write in accidentals. Chords in open spacing should be converted to close spacing in the scored versions, and octave doublings are to be added wherever appropriate. The chord members now in bass and soprano should be retained; for example, in the third chord below, a D (in whatever octave is desired) should be the bottom note, and a B should be the top note. In the exercises on page 36, an extra staff is provided as an aid in sketching the chords in advance.

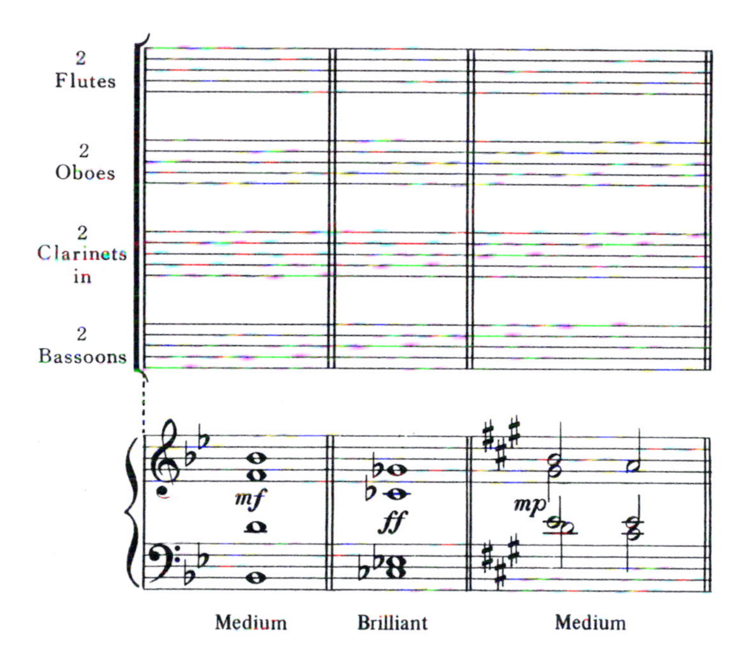

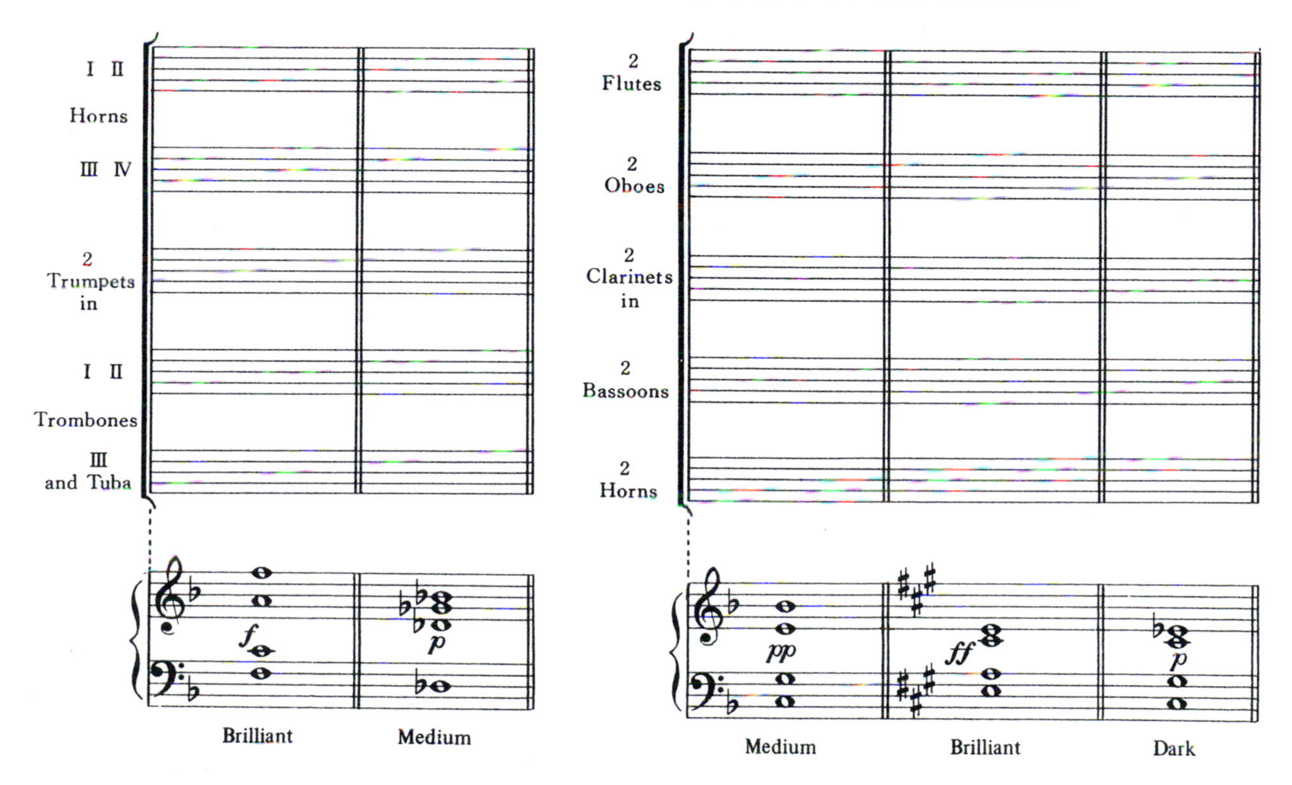

D. "Average" Orchestra
2 Flutes
2 Oboes
2 Clarinets in
2 Bassoons
I II
Horns
III IV
2 Trumpets in
I II
Trombones
III and Tuba
I
Violins
II
Violas
Cellos
Double Basses
f
mf
Brilliant
Dark
Medium
E. Large Orchestra
Piccolo
2 Flutes
2 Oboes
English Horn
2 Clarinets in
Bass Clarinet
2 Bassoons
Contra Bassoon
4 Horns
3 Trumpets in
I II
Trombones
III and Tuba
I
Violins
II
Violas
Cellos
Double Basses
mp
ff
Medium
Very brilliant

Score for strings (or for any other combination of instruments specified by the instructor). Rearrange, fill, etc. wherever appropriate. Include bowing indications.

This excerpt used by permission of Breitkopf & Haertel, Leipzig–Associated Music Publishers, Inc.

Score for strings (or for any other combination of instruments specified by the instructor). Rearrange, fill etc., wherever appropriate. Include bowing indications.

Score for strings. Rearrange, fill, etc. wherever appropriate. Include bowing indications.

SONATA, OP. 22

Beethoven

In planning the scoring, take into account the antiphonal effect at the beginning.

Fl.
Ob.
Clar.
Bsns.
I
Vl.
II
Vla.
Vc.
D. B.
dolce
espr.
dimin.
ritard.
pp
etc.

Score for woodwinds, horns, and strings. In the repeat of the first 12 measures, vary the scoring and add upper-octave doublings. From measure 33 on, partially fill in the wide gap between the hands. This piece is also suitable as an exercise in scoring for an orchestra that includes full brass and timpani.

Score the excerpt below in four different ways (versions 3 and 4 on the reverse side). Use only the instruments desired in each version—except for number 4, which is to use all the instruments listed. Include octave doublings of the melody in at least two versions. In addition to these actual scorings, describe two other possible scorings in the space provided on the next page.

NOCTURNE, Op. 55, No. 1 (continued)

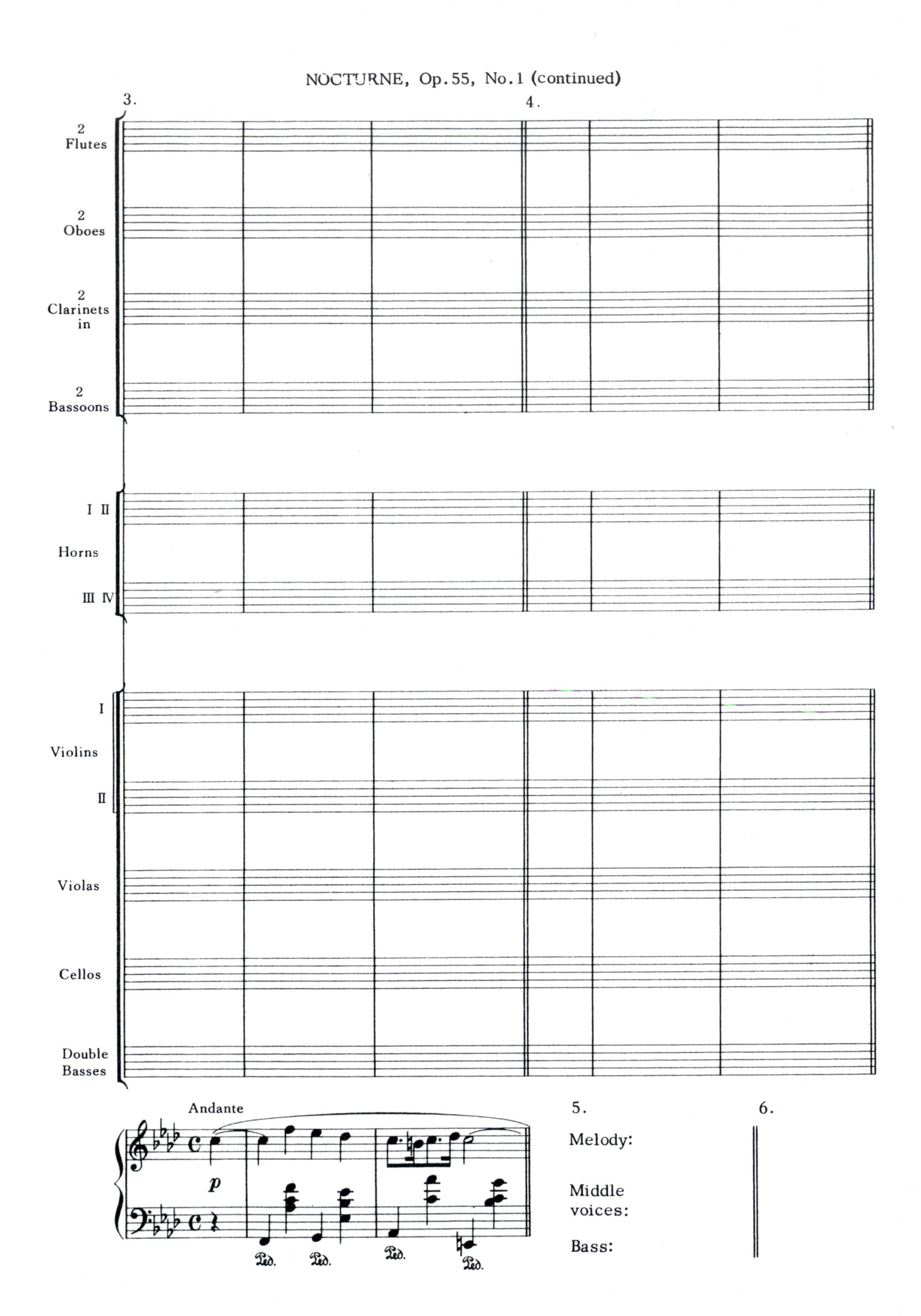

Score for woodwinds, horns if desired, and strings. The scoring should reflect the antiphonal character of the music.

Score for woodwinds in pairs, 4 horns, and strings.

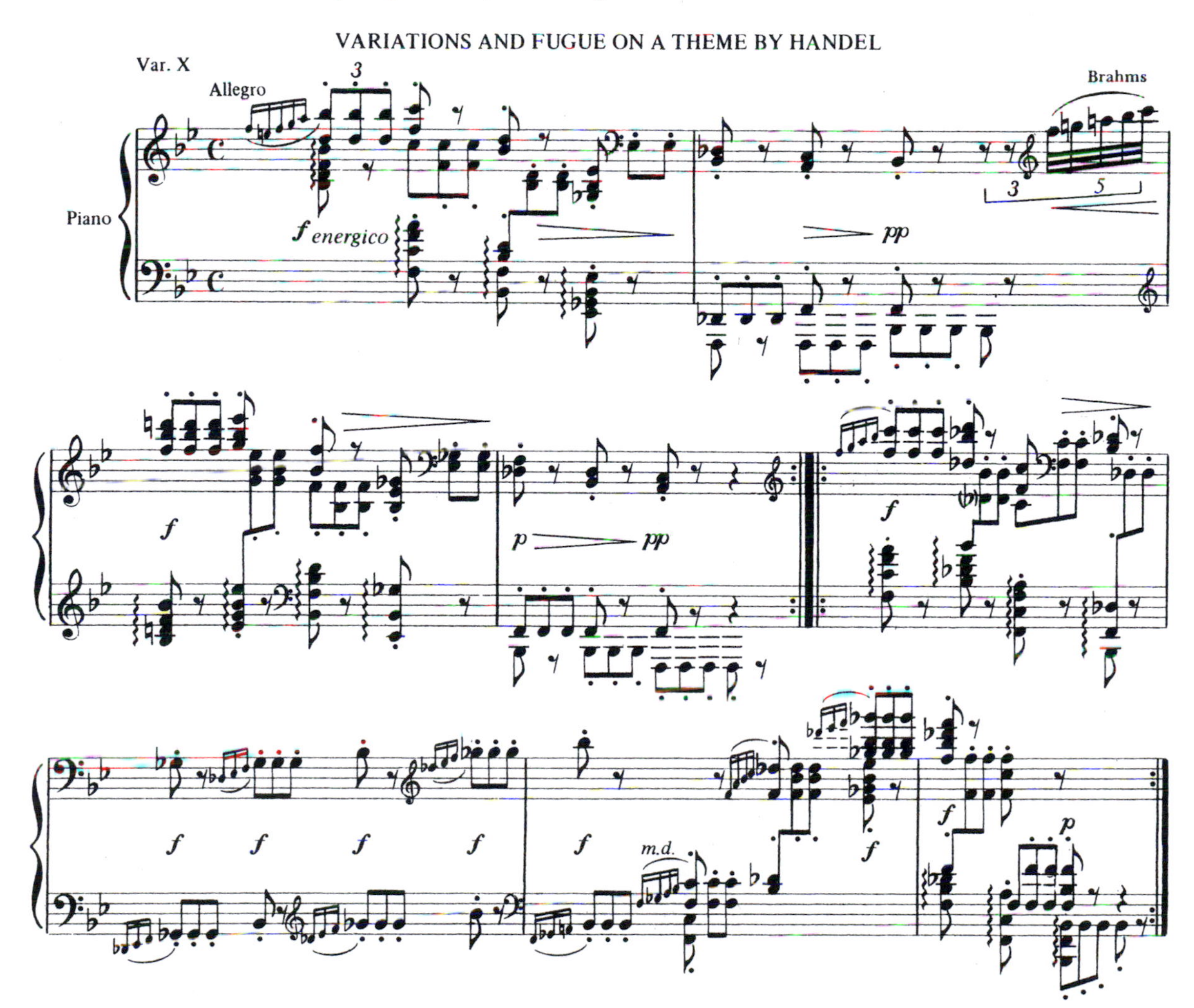

Score for woodwinds, horns if desired, and strings. From measure 13 on, there are good opportunities for changing colors and antiphonal effects.

This excerpt is also suitable for an assignment in scoring for woodwinds alone or strings alone, although neither group alone is as effective as a combination of the two.

1) Write a part for four timpani. For the initial tuning, try to select pitches that will fit into the harmonies throughout the piece (at the points where timpani are being used). If changes in tuning are felt to be necessary, remember to allow at least three or four measures of rest for each change and to indicate which timpano is to be changed.

2) The second blank staff may be used either for a part for one or more other percussion instruments or for another (alternative) timpani part. The instructor should specify which of these is to be done.

3) This music may also be used as the basis for an assignment in scoring for woodwinds, horns, and strings or for full orchestra.

IMPORTANT EVENT

IMPORTANT EVENT, continued

The instructor is to specify in which of the following ways the next excerpt is to be used:

a) Imagine that the music is to be scored for orchestra and write parts here for at least four percussion instruments. Except for those of definite pitch, two instruments may be written on the same staff if necessary.

b) On another sheet, actually score the music for orchestra and include parts for at least four percussion instruments.

The instructor is to specify in which of the following ways these excerpts are to be used:

a) Imagine that the music is to be scored for orchestra and write parts here for at least four percussion instruments. Except for those of definite pitch, two instruments may be written on the same staff if necessary.

b) On another sheet, actually score the music for orchestra and include parts for at least four percussion instruments.

MARCH

From "The Love of Three Oranges"

Tempo di marcia

Prokofieff

Piano

p

sempre staccato

etc.

Piano

ff

etc.

REWRITING EXERCISES FOR HARP

Rewrite the following passages for harp in such way as to involve the fewest possible pedal changes. Do not omit notes but change spellings where that will eliminate pedal changes. Include a pedal setting at the beginning of each exercise and indicate pedal changes as they occur. Each of these exercises can be rewritten so as to require only one pedal change.

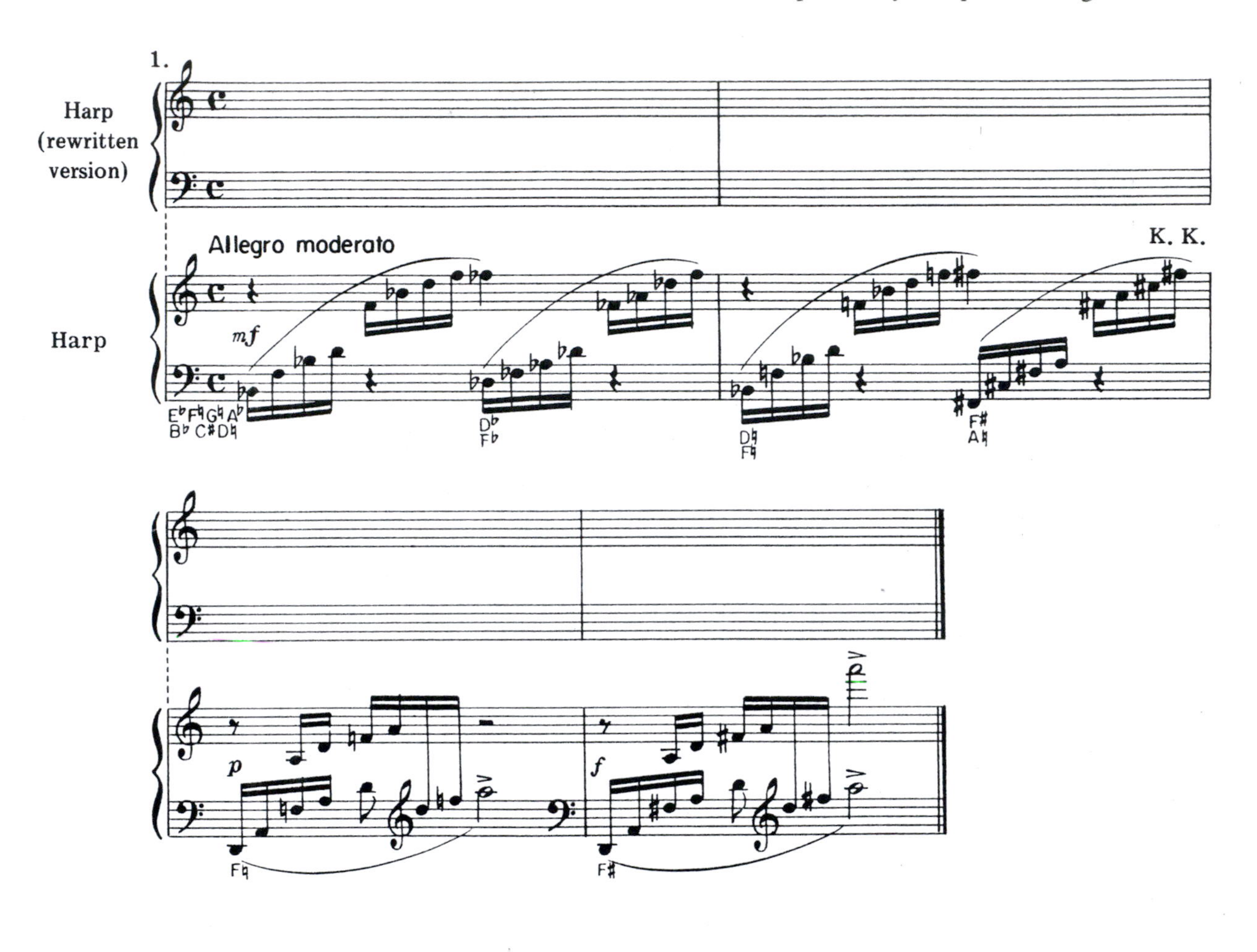

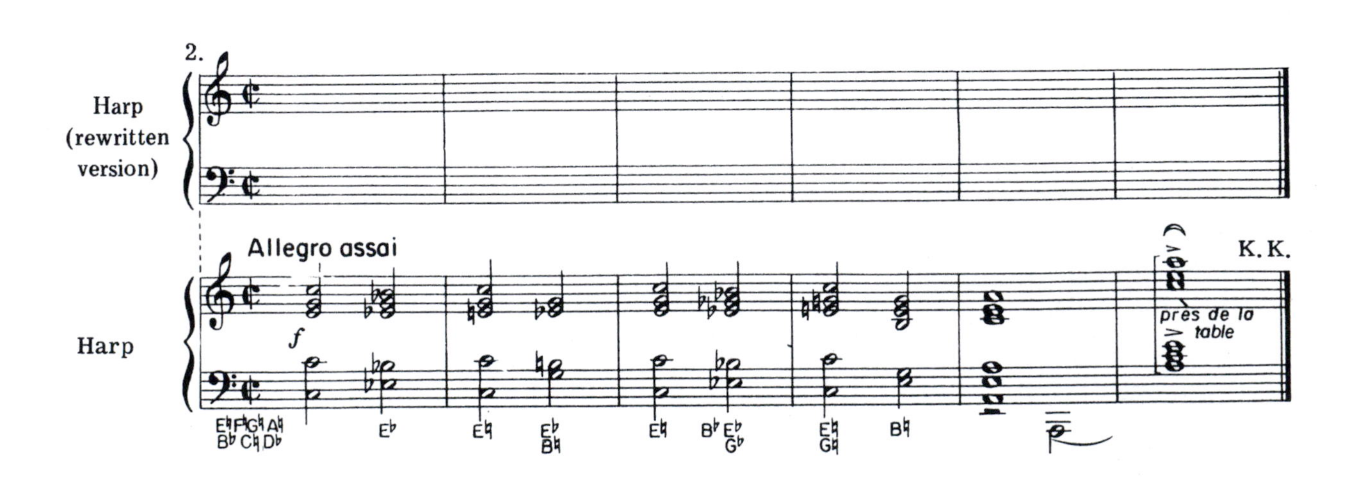

HARP EXERCISES

In Exercises 1 and 2, rewrite (respell) the passages in such a way as to involve the fewest possible pedal changes. Include a pedal setting at the beginning of each exercise and indicate pedal changes as they occur. These exercises can be rewritten so as to require only two and four pedal changes, respectively.

In Exercise 3, add the appropriate accidentals to the letters given below each chord to show the pedal setting that would be needed if the chord were to be played as a glissando on the harp. Also show each pedal setting in diagram form.

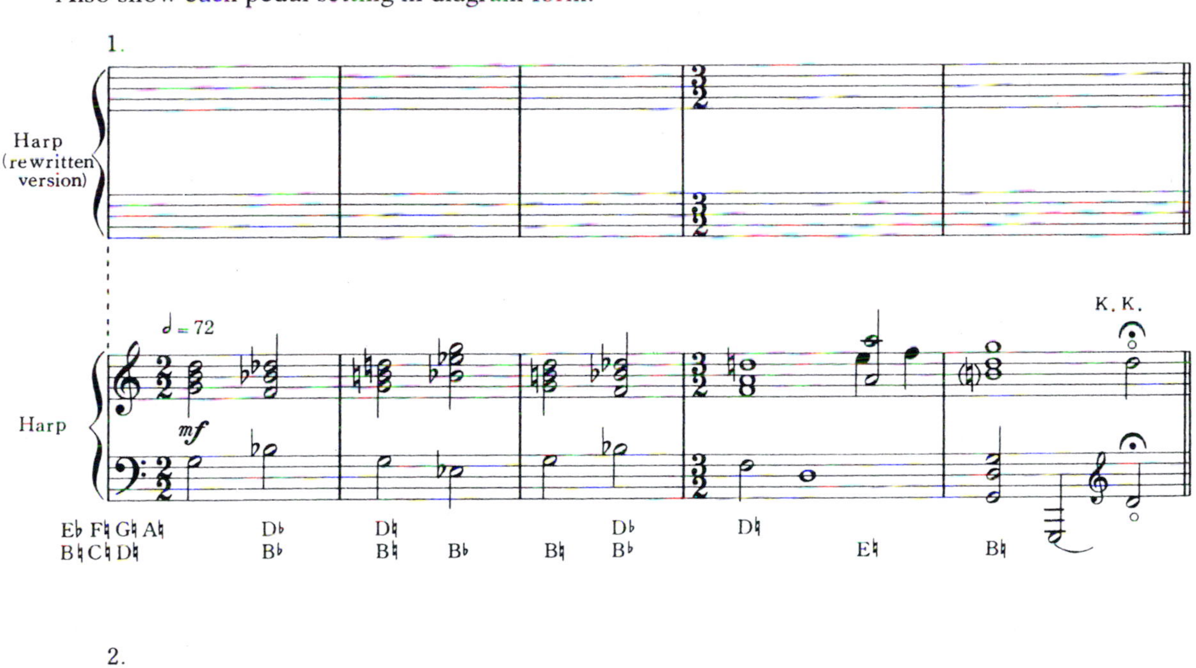

Score for woodwinds, horns, and strings, plus percussion—and harp if desired. Meter changes must be inserted at the actual measures where they occur. This piece is also suitable for an assignment in scoring for strings alone.

NO. 12 From FIFTEEN HUNGARIAN PEASANT SONGS

Allegretto (♩ = 112)

Bartók

Piano

leggiero

sfp

sf *sempre* **p**

sf

più **p**

pp

calando

1

etc.

Score for orchestra. Aim for maximum brilliance and fullness.

CRUSADERS' HYMN

EXERCISE IN ERROR DETECTION (SCORING FOR ORCHESTRA)

Leaving aside questions of stylistic appropriateness, point out, on this page or on a separate sheet, errors or instances of questionable scoring in the following. Alternatively, this exercise may be done orally in class.

Score for orchestra. Harp may be included but should not be depended upon entirely for the rolled chords; strings should also take them.

This piece is also suitable for an assignment in scoring for woodwinds, horns, and strings.

Score for a "Schumann" orchestra: woodwinds in pairs, 4 horns, 2 trumpets, 2 trombones, timpani and strings. Use all the instruments in the first 8 measures (and later if desired). The gaps in the open-spaced harmonies at the start may be filled in where that seems desirable, whereas the closely-spaced chords in the left hand (measures 10, 11, etc.) should be respaced so as to be less muddy. In measure 17, consider the effect of the pedal.

FANTASIA, OP. 17

Score for orchestra.

Score for orchestra. Note particularly the differences in dynamics that are called for.

BAGATELLE No. 1
from
TEN BAGATELLES, OP. 5

Tcherepnine

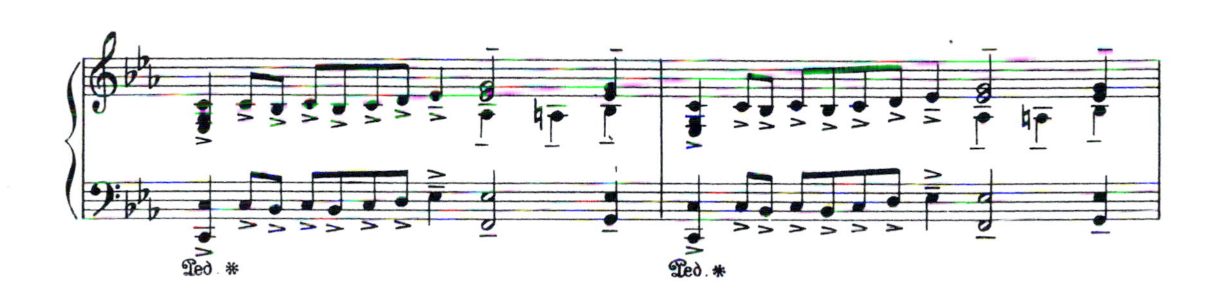

p sempre
Ped. *
una corda

Ped. *

Ped. *
Ped. *

8
p
sf
f
sf
ff
Ped.
*
Ped. * Ped. *
Ped

Score for orchestra (or only woodwinds, horns and strings plus harp, if desired). Note the effect of the pedal indications, especially in the closing measures of the excerpt.

NOTTURNO.

p a tempo.
poco
Ped.
p
poco
Ped.
Più mosso.
pp
Ped. una corda
Ped.
ppp
poco a poco
cresc.
Ped.
molto
Ped. tre corde
ff
Ped.
poco rit.
etc.

Score for an orchestra consisting of woodwinds in pairs, 2 horns, 2 trumpets, 3 trombones, 2 timpani, and strings.

Score for voice and an orchestra consisting of 1 flute, 1 oboe, 1B♭ clarinet, 1 bassoon, 1 horn, 1 trumpet (C), 1 trombone, harp, and a string section of about 10, 8, 6, 4, 2 (the instrumentation used by the composer in scoring this work.) If possible, the instructor should obtain the score (*Eight Poems of Emily Dickinson*) so that students may compare their completed scores with Copland's.

To Marcelle de Manziarly

5. Heart, we will forget him

Music by
AARON COPLAND

* Grace note on the beat

moving forward
When you have done, pray tell me,
Ped. sim.
faster
rit. e dim. (gradual
That I my thoughts may dim
molto marc.
return to a tempo)
Haste lest while you're lag - ging, I
may re - mem - ber him.

EXERCISES IN SCORING IN THE STYLES OF DEBUSSY AND STRAUSS

These fragments attempt to imitate the musical styles of Debussy and Strauss, respectively, and were written expressly to serve as exercises in orchestrating in the manner of these composers. That is, Exercise 1 is to be scored as Debussy might have scored it, Exercise 2 as Strauss might have scored it. This assignment obviously assumes a previous study of orchestral works of these composers.

Octave doublings may be used wherever they seem appropriate. The instrumentation chosen in each case should be typical of that employed by the composer whose style is being imitated.

Score for orchestra. Analyze first, marking appearances of the subject (or answer). Although no dynamics are included in the original, they must be supplied in the score. This fugue is most often played at a tempo of about 𝅗𝅥 = 58–60.

FUGUE VII
(WELL TEMPERED CLAVIER, Volume II)

J.S. Bach

Score for orchestra.

sostenuto sempre
p
calando
p
pp
Ped.
Ped.simile
poco rit. . . . . a tempo
energico
f
p mezza voce
etc.

Score for orchestra. Because of the many departures from the key signature in this composition, it will probably prove easiest to write the orchestral score without a key signature, accidentals being inserted instead. Compare your completed scoring with the published orchestral version.

This music is also suitable for an assignment in scoring for woodwinds, horns, and strings (plus harp, celesta, or any other instruments desired).

pp
3
3
5
5
Con languore
p
poco affrett.
p esitando
affrett.
mf
f
affrett.
f dim.

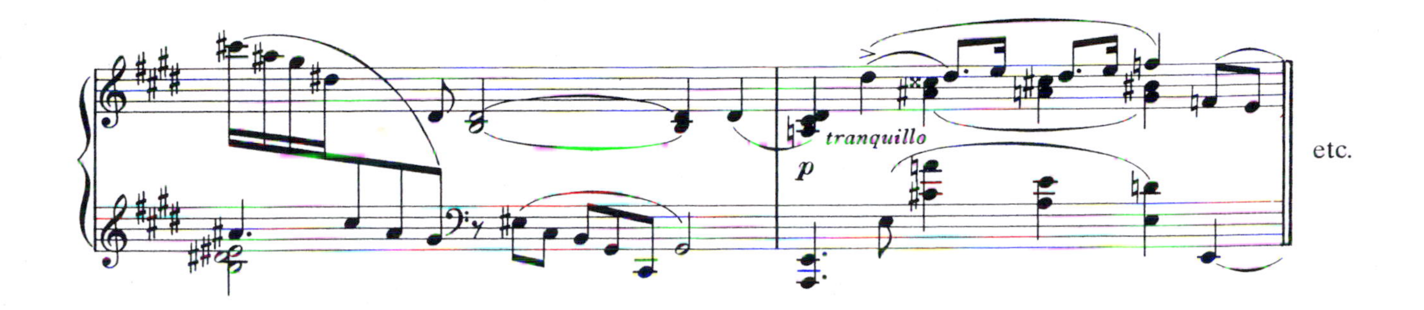

Score for orchestra. The first half of this piece, orchestrated by the composer, is given in Chapter 11 of the text (5th ed.). Compare your completed scoring with that.

This piece is also suitable for an assignment in scoring for: 1) woodwinds plus extra woodwinds and/or horns; 2) woodwinds, horns, and strings.

BAGATELLE 8. From Twelve Bagatelles

Score for orchestra. Make some use of special color effects (percussion, harp or piano, etc.)

MARCH, OP. 12, No. 1

Prokofieff

fz
fz
fz
fz
f
fz
fz
fz
3
8
fz
3
8
Some 32 measures, involving the repetition of themes already stated, are omitted here. The closing measures of the piece follow.
8
brillante
8
fff
p subito

e for high school orchestra, transposing the piece to another key to avoid the six-flat key nature in the second section and to allow for more resonance and easier fingering in the trings throughout. Include cues where that seems advisable (see Chapter 19 in the text). Or, score for a symphony orchestra, retaining the original key if desired.

GOLLIWOGG'S CAKE WALK

from
"The Children's Corner"

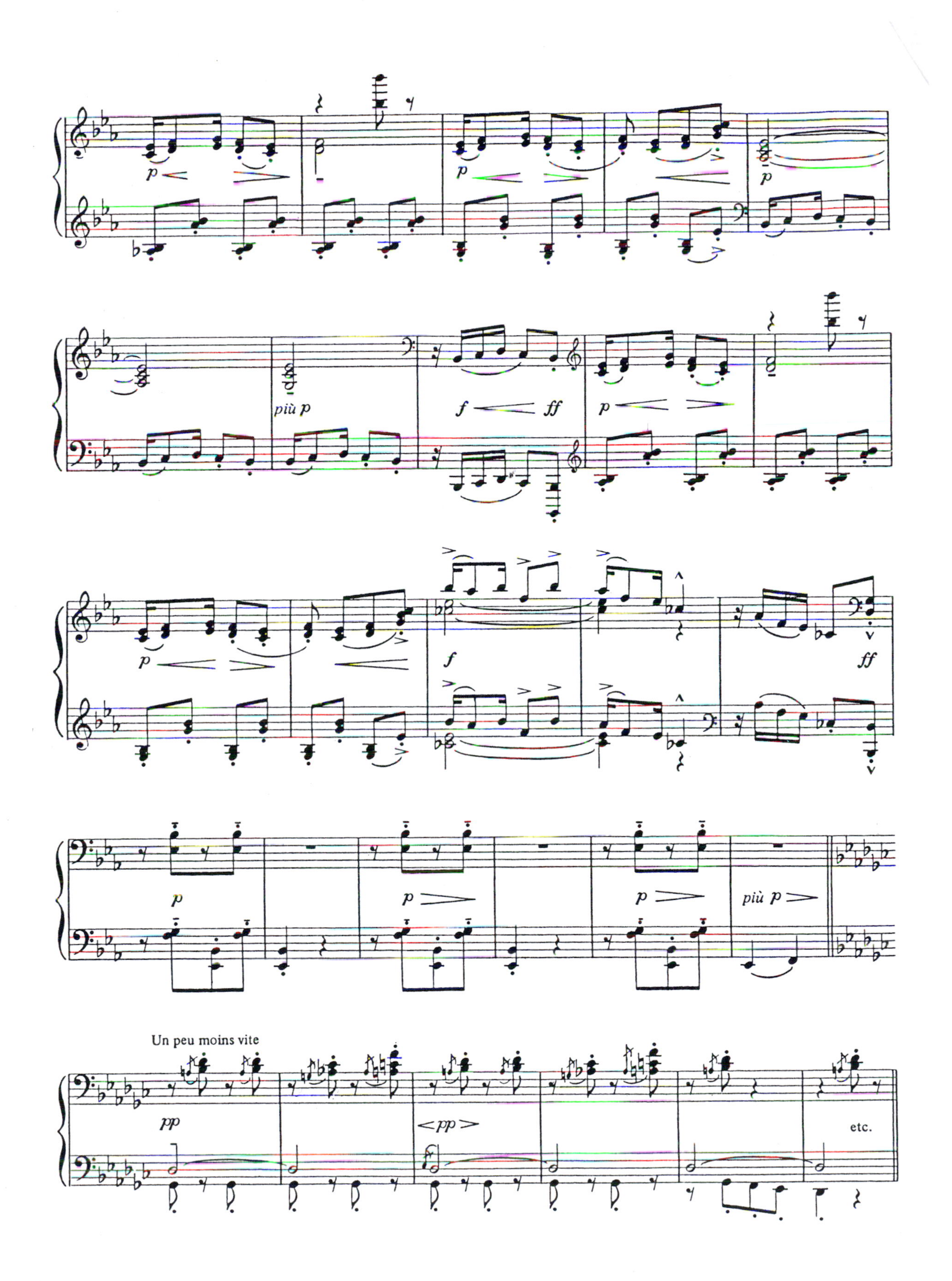

p
p
p
più p
f
ff
p
p
f
ff
p
p
p
più p
Un peu moins vite
pp
pp
etc.